LOOK

AT

MY

GOD! 4

(Victories in Evangelism Santa Cruz journey)

Pastor Paul M. Caprietta

Look at My God! 4
Victories in Evangelism
Santa Cruz Journey
By Pastor Paul M. Caprietta
Copyright © 2019

ISBN:9798657501766

Published by Pastor Paul M. Caprietta
Pico Rivera, California
www.divineministriesinc.org

Printed in the United States of America

Foundational Scriptures

"I thank Christ Jesus our Lord, who has given me strength; that he considered me trustworthy, appointed me into service. Even though I was once a blasphemer and a persecutor, and a violent man. I was shown mercy because I acted in ignorance and unbelief. The grace of our Lord was poured out on me abundantly, along with the faith and love that are in Christ Jesus.

1 Timothy 1:12-14

"Then I heard the voice of the Lord saying, who shall I send? And who will go for us? And I said, "Here am I, send me!"

Isaiah 6:8

"For when I preach the gospel, I cannot boast, since I am compelled to preach. Woe to me if I do not preach the gospel."

1 Corinthians 9:16

Preface

I wrote this life-changing and inspirational book to document twelve additional evangelistic experiences I have had along my journey in ministry for the past twenty-six years. I have strong anointed upon my life to lead people into a real and dynamic relationship with Jesus Christ is this is evident in the stories listed in this book. I met so many interesting and yet people living with so many challenges that it was incumbent upon me t document their stories for people to glean by.

I have such a desire to see people live to their greatest potential in life and therefore, I am moved with compassion to afford them this journey of life blessings and victories in life. God has tremendously blessed me to a conduit to flow his blessings to other people and I am so mindful for the grace and mercy he has bestowed upon me that I cannot stand still and see people having any direction in life.

I have noticed so many Christians reluctant to share the gospel of Jesus Christ with others for reasons I am very disappointed and annoyed by. I will take the opportunity to list some reasons believers in Christ stated for fear of sharing the gospel with others. With so many bad news being reported in the world, why would Christians hesitant in sharing some good news with people. Some of the reasons are mentioned below.

Firstly, some describe of fear of being rejected by people. Secondly, do not like talking to people and thirdly, fear of not knowing the Bible in its entirety and fourthly satan fulling their minds with fear of making them afraid of people challenging them with the contents of the Bible.

My desire in writing this book is to jumpstart your faith into reaching out to people by sharing the good news of Jesus Christ with others. People are dying and without making Jesus Christ as your personal savior, the reality is that they will not enter the kingdom of heaven.

I am reminded of the teachings found in the Bible.

The word of God says,

"*Jesus said to them, "Go into all the world and preach the gospel to all creation."*

Mark 16:15

The word of God said, go and the word go is an action word which means to do something to achieve a result. The question I am asking you my reader, are you being obedient to the call of God by being true to the instructions of our savior. We are required to do our part in being obedient to God and allow God's Holy Spirit to work through us.

Trust me, you will get the results if you are obedient to the one who commissioned you into service and complete His work. I am an example of being obedient to the work of the Lord.

The Bible teaches,

"Don't you know that when you offer yourselves to someone as obedient slaves, you are slaves of the one you obey-whether you are slaves to sin, which leads to death, or to obedience, which leads to righteousness?"

Romans 6:16

Contents

Who Should read this book?

Anyone desiring to jump-start their faith and start ministering to people. God has placed an enormous responsibility on His children and do the work of an evangelist, but unfortunately so many believers in Christ has being stuck in a spirit of complacency and as a result curtails the growing of the ministry hear in earth. We must stop "playing church" and continue ministering to the needs of people.

As believers in Christ, we should be looking for ways to reach out to others, so they come into a true and mature relationship with Jesus Christ, the only true and living God. People are hurting and in need of someone who can offer them hope and steer them in the direction of the true savior. We are living in a challenging and sometimes callous world and people desperately need hope.

Jesus Christ came into the world to save that which was lost, and we were all lost prior to accepting Jesus Christ as our savior. In addition, he came to set the captives free and we as believers in Christ must do whatever it takes to help set them free and help advance the kingdom of god on the earth.

If you are truly willing to lead people into a closer relationship with Jesus Christ take time to pray and seek the Lord and be moved by the Spirit of compassion. I do not have any formula for leading people to Jesus Christ, but I depend on the Spirit of God for wisdom, knowledge and understanding. May the Spirit of the living God fall upon you my reader, and may you lead people to Jesus Christ in a greater dimension. Ministering and winning people to Jesus Christ brings joy to the person sharing the gospel and to the person accepting the Lord. This process brings to two-fold blessing to both parties. Get the program now people of the living God.

The Bible clearly teaches,

"How, then, can they call on the one they have not believed in? And how can they believe in the one of whom they have not heard? And how can they hear without someone preaching to them."

Romans 10:14

Someone needs to go so that people can hear the gospel of Jesus Christ. We are commissioned by our Heavenly father to be obedient to the call of sharing the gospel with people we meet. The scripture is very straight forward for everyone to understand.

Introduction

Introduction
How it started

I received a phone call on one sunny Saturday afternoon in the month of July 2016 from a young lady. The name and number showed up on my caller ID as Gail. I answered the call and the person said is this "Rev. Paul Caprietta," and I said yes and who am I speaking too. She said, "my name is Gail and I was a co-worker at a school in Trinidad where we both teach from 1985 thru 1989 and do you remember me?" I said yes, I do.

She said, "I was browsing the internet for you and your name came up as Re. Paul Caprietta and she further irritated, I so surprised that you are a pastor now and I remembered you telling us in the school office in 1998 that you will become a Pastor one day preaching the word of God and we all laughed at you making such a statement because we thought it was funny, seeing the lifestyle you were presently living."

When my wife, Gail came home from work I shared with her the conversation I just had from a past co-worker of mine many years ago while living and working at a school in Trinidad. She was utterly amazed by what I said. I told Gail, my wife, I recalled making that statement in the summer of 1998 while working at that school in Trinidad as a Computer Science lecturer. Some of the staff members were sitting in the school office talking about different topics about school, family and life. When suddenly I said to my co-workers that I will be a Pastor one day.

I did not know why I made that statement; however, I believe it was the call of God upon my life that allow that statement to come out of my mouth. I was not even a Christian at that time, but God knew I am one of His chosen servants to proclaim the gospel of Jesus Christ to a lost and dying world. A year later in 1989, I left that Institution for another one and while working at the new Institution I accepted Jesus Christ as my personal savior and Lord, all to the glory of God.

On the morning of September 18, 2016 my wife and I was talking about the goodness f God upon our lives when I called Gail, my past co-worker and she shared the same information with my wife Gail, that I made in the year 1988. God is truly an awesome God.

The Bible declares,

"Before I formed you in the womb, I knew you, before you were born, I set you apart; I appointed you as a prophet to the nations."

Jeremiah 1:5

To my surprise, I received a phone call form Gail, my former co-worker on Saturday 29 July 2017. We spoke about life in Trinidad and generally how things are going on with each other, when suddenly I felt an unction from the Holy Spirit to share the gospel of Jesus Christ with her. The word of God went forth with clarity and purpose and she subsequently said, "yes to Jesus Christ as her personal savior and Lord." She was very excited to accept Jesus Christ as her personal savior and Lord. She further, reminded me that, "I can call her anytime so we can pray together."

I was very overwhelmed by her remarks of saying that I can call her and pray anytime. God is truly an awesome, loving and compassionate God to whomever decides to accept Him as their personal savior and Lord. Gail my wife and Gail my fellow co-worker are partially responsible for me writing this life-changing and inspirational book for people to be motivated to fulfil the call of God upon their lives and win the lost for Jesus Christ.

The Bible teaches,

"The fruit of the righteous is a tree of life, and the one who is wise saves lives."

Proverbs 11:30

We keep in touch on a regular basis, we spoke on August 20, 2019 and I told her to keep sharing the good news of Jesus Christ and she said, "I will because God has been good to me." I was so elated to hear her determination to do what is good and obedient to His will. I praise God for her life.

Chapter 1

The twelve Workings

Chapter 1
The twelve Workings

I have decided to write part 4, of this book because I realized there are so many more scenarios that needed to document to allow people to start fulfilling the great commission and complete this great work God has called us to do on the earth. I will document twelve additional experiences that will bless your life tremendously.

The number twelve represents a perfect number. It symbolizes God's power and authority. When Jesus Christ went to hell, He took the keys of death and He gave that power and authority to the church, which is Christ body on the earth.

The Bible teaches,

"I will give you the keys of the kingdom of heaven; whatever you bind on earth will be bound in heaven, and whatever you lose on earth will be loosed in heaven."

Matthew 16:19

"The sting of death is sin, and the power of sin is the law."

1 Corinthians 15:56

The number twelve is the number of perfection as mentioned above. That was the reason Jesus Chose twelve disciples because He chose twelve men to change the world, and we are his disciples bringing salvation to the whole world for those who accept Him as their personal savior and Lord.

The word salvation in the Greek language is "SOZO" which means completely whole. Jesus Christ gave us the power and authority so that, we can help make us, his people completely whole in Him. We serve a prefect and glorious God, willing that none should perish but all come into the knowledge of the truth.

The Bible teaches,

"The Lord will vindicate; your love, Lord, endures forever-do not abandon the works of your hands."

Psalm 138:8

We are His disciples because we are His followers, students and joint heirs with Him bringing hope to a lost and dying world. We are His disciples and we must follow the commands and statures of God bringing light to a dark and callous world. I am one of His disciples who are working to accomplish the assignment God has called you and me to do which is to bring people into a closer relationship with Jesus Chris, our soon and coming King.

Throughout this book, you will have noticed the love and compassion I have shown to the people I brought into a closer relationship with Jesus Christ. It takes a lot of effort and lots of compassion to steer people to Jesus Christ. Remember, God is a God of compassion and He loves everyone. We as believers, of Jesus Christ must be aware that people need help and we must take every opportunity to provide that help that they need. I will now take the opportunity to list some significance of the number twelve.

Listed below are a few illustrations of the power use of the number twelve: -

- Jesus started His earthy ministry at twelve years old in the temple.
- Jesus originally had twelve disciples.
- There were twelve disciples.
- There were twelve apostles.
- There are twelve tribes of Israel.
- Twelve legions of angels.
- Jesus sitting upon twelve thrones.
- Judging the twelve tribes of Israel.
- In Orthodox Judaism twelve signifies the age a girl matures.
- There are twelve great feasts.
- In Hinduism, the sun god Surya has twelve names.
- There are twelve calendar months.
- There are twelve months in a year.
- There are generally twelve jurors.
- There are generally a twelve-step program to recovery.
- There are twelve Greek Gods and Goddesses

Therefore, based on the information listed above you can appreciate the importance of the number twelve both spiritually and the value society placed on the number twelve. Hence the reason I have decided to document twelve scenarios of my evangelistic outreaches for my reader to glean by and to complete the work God had commissioned all His disciples. God is calling everyone of us to do the work of an evangelist with a spirit of joy and gladness knowing that we are doing a great and mighty work for the Lord.

The scripture teaches,

"But you, keep your head in all situations, endure hardship, do the work of an evangelist, discharge all the duties of your ministry."

2 Timothy 4:5

Chapter 2

Lady in Distress

Chapter 2
Lady in Distress

Before I start documenting this scenario. My wife and I was invited to a conference in Northern California, Santa Cruz to be precise in December 2018. We decided to invite Gail's mother, which is my Mother-in-law. We rented a car and decided to drive to San Cruz, Northern California. Our journey started off at 9am on December 29, 2018. We parked our stuff and was on our way to Santa Cruz, we first drop off to get gasoline and the Lord used me to minister to the female gas station attendant about God. God is very much interested in her living a life of peace and comfort. She looked at me and said, "yes I know." I was not able to further minister to her because there were people in line waiting to pay for gasoline as well and we her hurrying to get to our destination in San Cruz about a six-hour drive from Los Angeles. We were very much aware that our check in at 6pm and we will have to stop off four our bathroom breaks.

I was so excited to start off sharing the good news with her but unfortunately, I was not able to lead her to Jesus Christ due to the reasons mentioned above, however I know the word of God went forth with power. The way the young lady looked at me I know I had some impact on her and because the word of God is so powerful and timely in and for every situation in life.

The Bible clearly states,

"So is my word that goes out from my mouth: it will not return to me empty but will accomplish what I desire and achieve the purpose for which I sent it."

Isaiah 55:11

I felt in my heart that I should have waited until everyone had paid and continue to share the good news with her. However, I know that God will work on her heart and God will send someone to complete the work that I have started in her life. I am reminded what the scripture teaches.

"I planted the seed, Apollos watered it, but god made it grow."

1 Corinthians 3:6

I pray to God that He uses someone anointed and full of the Holy Ghost to steer that young lady into a relationship of Jesus Christ as their personal savior and Lord.

I truly planted the seed of the good news and I believe God will send the right person at the right time to help that young lady. I am rooted for her salvation. Therefore, we continue our travel and we drove for two hours and landed in another city to purchase gasoline and stretched our legs and noticed a young man cleaning the counters at another gas station when the Lord gave me a word for this young man, which as very profound the way the Lord use me to share the gospel with him.

This scenario will be illustrated on the next chapter because is shows on coloration with the previous scenario.

Chapter 3

Unconditional Love

Chapter 3
Unconditional Love

This scenario is very much interesting and yet very profound because it illustrates the love of God towards mankind. As I walked into the service station, I saw a young man cleaning the countertop and said to him, you are doing a very good job in cleaning the countertop. He responded, by telling me that, "he loves having things look clean." I said, to him that is great news brother. He smiled, and I told him that Jesus Christ is interested in having your heart clean the way you are cleaning the countertop.

The way he looked at me and was a bit surprised by the statement coming out of my mouth. I further reiterated by asking him if he know Jesus Christ as his personal savior and Lord? He made a statement, by saying "we are all God's children and that we are all his people," which made me believe that he does not know Jesus Christ intimately as he should. I pressed him further and his statements was fizzled and confusing. The dialogue continues for an additional five to six minutes and I realized I was not getting anywhere with this young man.

On leaving I shared with him that God loves him dearly and if he takes the time to reflect on God's love it will be very rewarding for him. In addition, I informed him that the love of God will clean his heart the way he cleans the countertops for your employer. He looked and smile at me and I know that those statement penetrating his heart to the core. I told and share with him the following scriptures found in the Bible.

The Bible teaches,

"In reply Jesus declared, I tell you the truth, no one can see the kingdom of God unless he is born-again."

John 3:3

"For God so love the world that he gave his one and only son. That whoever believes in him shall not perish but have eternal life."

John 3:16

He said thanks, "for sharing your heart with me." I told him take care of yourself and be blessed. I do not know if I will ever see him again, however, God knows his heart's desire and god will use someone to lead him to Jesus Christ if he desires to have a real and intimate relationship with Jesus Christ. My reader, it means that minister to two people and neither of them accepted Jesus Christ as their personal savior. However, the word of God was shared with those two people. As mentioned above the word of God will not returned to him void but it will accomplish that which it was sent it out to do. I am encouraged as I continue my journey to Santa Cruz that souls will be saved, and lives will be transformed for the better.

The Bible teaches.

"He said to them, go into all the world and preach the good news to all creation."

Mark 16:15

I am being obedient and do what called me to do and encourage all my readers to do the same and help expand the kingdom of God on the earth.

Chapter 4

Concerned Personnel

Chapter 4
Concerned Personnel

Well, the conference stated in Santa Cruz, we arrived at about 5pm and had to wait for an hour for us to complete the check-in for the conference. We had dinner and late in the evening was the start of the conference with praise and Worship service which was spirit-filled, and the people were blessed.

On conclusion of the praise and worship service we were asked by the worship leader to introduce ourselves and get to know the names of a few people and get their contact information. While getting to know some people I was drawn to a young lady who seem to be very serious minded and yet discipline in the way she conducted herself. I was encouraged by my wife to share the gospel of Jesus Christ with her. Therefore, I took it upon myself to minister the gospel of Jesus Christ with her and she was, so it bit surprised that I am willing to minister the gospel with her because she attends church and she is attending a Christian conference

My brothers and sisters in Christ God are no respecter of person. They that call upon the name of the Lord will be saved. On conclusion of sharing the gospel with her she accepted Jesus Christ as her personal savior and Lord. We keep in touch via text messages and she was so delighted to accept Jesus Christ as her personal savior and Lord. She further shared with me, "she is believing God for a husband." I am believing God for a godly husband for her and that God will perfect everything that concerns her. This young lady came to the Christian conference for the last couple of years, attend church services on a regular basis and met me and accepted Jesus Christ as her personal savior and Lord. In my opinion, attending 2018 conference was the best conference she has attended because it brought her closer to Jesus Christ and gave her a new hope, purpose and reason to be the best person in live. When I see her at the 2019 conference we will reconnect in person and I am willing to impart some spiritual teachings in her life.

This seems as a surprise for the reasons mentioned above but we cannot take it for granted because someone attends church regularly and attend Christian conferences means that she is a Christian.

There are so many people that puts on the religious act and believe they are heaven bound. My reader, that is a dangerous position to be in.

The Bible teaches,

"*Jesus replied, truly I tell you, no one can see the kingdom of God unless they are born-again.*"

John 3:3

The Bible did not teach that you must be a church goer and be a nice person as the only criteria to enter the kingdom of heaven, but on the contrary, you must accept Jesus Christ as your personal savior and Lord. My reader, this is plain reality of life and if you accept Jesus Christ, live according to His commands and statures you are saved.

Chapter 5

The Nurse in Need

Chapter 5
The Nurse in Need

The next morning of the conference there was eight of us sitting around the table having breakfast and enjoying each other's companionship. It worked out that all of us sitting around the table were first time visitors at the conference, which gave us a comradery and a sense of being unique and being a fist time attendee at the conference in common with each other. We all introduced ourselves and who invite each one to the conference.

With me I am always looking for ways to be a blessing to people spiritually. I asked people around the table a very poignant question about their salvation experience, when we reach to the last person, who is a nurse she said, "I do not know Jesus Christ as my personal savior and Lord?" I took the opportunity and shared with her the gospel and the importance of living for Jesus Christ.

I shared with her she helped people with their physical well-being, and I want to introduce you to a person who can offer you spiritual well-being, which in my opinion was a game changer and it got her attention. We must be led by the spirit of God to use engaging words to get people's attention.

After sharing the gospel with her, I asked her if she will like to accept Jesus Christ as her personal savior and Lord? She said, "yes" and was led to the Lord by praying the salvation prayer while having breakfast. All of us around the table encouraged her by praying the salvation prayer which gave her a sense of belonging. The word of God came with power and she accepted Jesus Christ as her personal savior and Lord.

It does not matter where I am, once the Holy Spirit give me the unction and the opportunity to do the work of the Him, I will do it to the best of my ability. God wants His people to be obedient and do the work of an evangelist and fulfill the great commission on the earth. I am reminded of the scripture found in the Holy Bible.

The Bible teaches,

"For he says, In the time of my favor I heard you, and in the day of Salvation I helped you." I tell you, now is the time of God's favor, now is the day of Salvation."

2 Corinthians 6:2

We keep in touch with each other occasionally and it is always a blessing to hear that she is doing much better. I encouraged her in the commands and statures of God, and I pray that she will be used mightily of find to bring others into a relationship with Jesus Christ. God loves His people unconditionally and He will be there at our side to provide comfort to us. The important concept to understand is that, God is willing to be a friend that sticks closer than a brother and to provide that necessary peace and strength to his people.

Chapter 6
The Worshipper

Chapter 6
The Worshipper

The next day for lunch we were all relaxing and reminiscing about the conference thus far, and we were sharing about what stand out most to each of us about the conference and what topics we will like to see for next year's conference. We were excited about meeting one of the attendees our friend invited and the churches he had visited so far. He said, "to us what he like most about churches that are attended and led by African American is the way they worship and praise God."

We shared with him that we attend a church that is led and directed by African American and we will like him to come and visit the church we attend. We were so excited to hear him say that he will like to attend one day, because he likes the way "black churches worship and their style of music." I mentioned to him that we will welcome his visit and he will enjoy our church style of worship and he was elated to know that the invitation is open for him to attend.

I felt his sincerity of heart in loving our style of worship and I took the time to ask him a very poignant question, which is do you know Jesus Christ as his personal savior and Lord? He responded by saying, "no I do not know him as my personal savior and Lord." I ask him do you want to know Jesus Christ as your personal savior and Lord. He responded by saying, "yes." I prayed with him on the table while having lunch and he was led to the Lord as his personal savior. I saw his expression after praying the Salvation prayer.

The Bible teaches,

"He then brought them out and asked, "Sirs, what must I do to be saved." They replied, "believe in the Lord Jesus, and you will be saved -you and your household."

Acts 16:30-31

"Consequently, faith comes from hearing the message, and the message is heard through the word of Christ."

Romans 10:17

I thank God for this young man Salvation experience and trusting God He will be a man on fire because for his love in enjoying worshipping God.

Chapter 7

Hovering person

Chapter 7
Hovering Person

This young man was very interesting and yet very profound in my opinion because it strikes a spirit of connection between two of us. I am African American, and the young man being white, but God is no respecter of person. As my wife, myself and my mother-in-law sit on the table to have our meals, this young white guy will come to our table to serve us and no other table he was willing to be a server.

This strike my attention and I mentioned it to my wife, and it spike their curiosity as well. I said to myself next mealtime I will take the opportunity to minister the gospel of Jesus Christ with him. Our next mealtime he showed up at our table to be our server and I said yes Lord this is his day and time for his Salvation. When he came to our table, we exchange pleasantries, and he was a very nice young man and it make it very easy to minister the gospel of Jesus Christ with him. We did not have much time because he was working. I said, to him I will like to talk to you, he said, "okay give me a moment." I said to him sure and we walked a few feet from the table.

I asked him, do you know Jesus Christ as your personal savior and Lord? He said, "no." I further asked him will you like to know Jesus Christ as your personal savior and Lord, because he can give you peace, strength and wisdom in whatever situation you are going through and he was delighted to know that accepting Jesus can do all these wonderful things for him, and that brought joy to this young man's life.

The Bible teaches,

"And everyone who calls on the name of the Lord will be saved."

Acts 2:21

This young man truly called upon the name of the Lord and he is saved by the grace of Almighty God. I asked him where do you live? he said, "Denver, Colorado." I shared with him to pray, read your Bible everyday and God will do a tremendous work in his life. He was so elated, and I saw it in his expression on his face. This young man came from Denver, Colorado to get saved.

What an awesome God we serve, who cares deeply about every challenge that we go through. Unfortunately, I did not get his telephone number to keep in touch with him however, God knows him, and God will work on his behalf. I am trusting God, for his victory and he will share the good news with other people he encounters in his daily walk.

We must be people that are willing to go out of our way to be a blessing to other. My reader, I was having dinner, however I was willing to interrupt my dinner to be a blessing to someone and to secure their heavenly home. I know God is well pleased with my decision and being of assistance to this young man and may God eternally secure his future in life. The question I am asking you, my reader, are you willing to be interrupted for the gospel sake or is it just about your desire in life.

The Bible teaches,

"But seek first his kingdom and his righteousness, and all these things will be given to you as well."

Matthew 6:33

Chapter 8

Outreach 1

Chapter 8
Outreach 1

I had a very interesting conversation with an elderly man a couple of months ago I shared a few stories about my evangelistic work, and he was fascinated about the work I do for the Lord. He asked me a very interesting question about leading people to Jesus Christ. The question he asked is, "do you lead everyone to Christ you minister to." I respond with a resounding no as my answer, he was a bit taken back to know my answer.

I said to him, brother it involves a lot of dedication and discipline to do this work, because you have to pray that God prepare the hearts of men and women to receive the gospel of Jesus Christ and you have to be willing to be transparent with people because some people can see straight through you if you are a fake. I thank my God, that no one have ever mentioned to me that I am a fake, I have heard a lot of edacious things from people on my twenty-six years in ministry.

The Bible teaches,

"As Long as it is day, we must do the works of him who sent me. Night is coming, when no one can work."

John 9:4

I am mindful of the fact that we are commissioned to do the work of God and to do it to best of our ability and let do his work, by convicting people of their sins and bring them into a closer relationship with Jesus Christ, our soon and coming King of Kings and Lord of Lords.

After dinner one day of the conference my wife and I decided to do "some our time," so we took a tour of the conference grounds. After looking at some of the conference grounds we went into the conference office and met one of the reservation clerks, who was very polite and professional, which are good quality traits that people should desire.

I took the time to introduce myself and my wife, and while chatting, asked her my signature question, do you know Jesus Christ as your personal savior and Lord? She responded by saying, "yes I know him." I further, question her about Jesus Christ and her answers were good and I thank God for her life in knowing the Lord Jesus Christ, which brought a sense of happiness.

On conclusion of the conversation my wife asked her how far it is from the beach? She gave us very precise directions and how to get to the beach and that was a blessing for my wife because she loves the beach the water because she is a water aerobics instructor.

Chapter 9

Jesus Loves you

Chapter 9
Jesus Loves you

Well, the conference came to a climax and it was a spirit-filled program where people were blessed, and I believe the people were challenged in living godly lives unto our heavenly father. On leaving the conference, in Santa Cruz to travel back home, we stopped off at the local beach and it was a pleasant scenery in looking at the water and the trees. I did not want to stay to long at the beach because the distance was a way off to get to our home.

On our journey home after two hours of driving we stop off at a service station to use the restrooms and stretch our legs. As I walked into the service station, I glazed my eyes upon a young man who was a service station attendant. I said, to him in a very bold manner, do you know Jesus Christ as your personal savior and Lord, if you do not know him, I come to lead you to Jesus Christ. I saw it in his face that He was a bit surprised, to know that someone can be so bold to share that with him.

I further asked him because of limited time, do you want to accept Jesus Christ as his savior and he responded, by saying "yes" and we prayed the Salvation prayer for him to come into a real acceptance of Jesus Christ. I did not take his telephone number for us to communicate with each other, but God will do his work in this young man's life.

The Bible explicitly states,

"The wicked flee through no one pursues, but the righteous are as bold as a Lion."

Proverbs 28:1

I am bold in sharing the gospel with others, because I feel in my heart that I am under obligation to do this work. God has done so much for me, therefore, it is only compassionate on me to do the same to help other enjoy this awesome experience of knowing Jesus Christ. I feel so frustrated with fellow Christians resist sharing the gospel for reasons mentioned above in my introduction in this life-changing and inspirational book.

Chapter 10
Clean Hearts

Chapter 10
Clean Hearts

This scenario is one of my best and most up most inspirational on our trip in my opinion because it showed the spirit of boldness, word of wisdom and most importantly, the gift of compassion towards the lost souls of the world. God is a great and awesome God who is willing that all come into a relationship with him and live their lives for him.

We have been driving now for another two hours and we needed a bathroom break and a stretch of our limbs. We stop off at one of the assigned rest stops and I noticed a custodian about the clean the men bathrooms. I asked him if it was okay for me to use it quickly, "he said yes sir go ahead and use it because I am to close if for cleaning." I was a bit happy because you know when you desperately need to use it, you have use it.

I was very impressed by his level of compassion towards me. While using the restroom and looked and him and felt the Lord wanted me to minister the love of Jesus Christ to him. I took God unction seriously and shared the good news with him. He received it with clarity, and I further asked him if we will like to accept Jesus Christ as his personal savior and Lord. He responded by saying, "yes sir."

I prayed with him the salvation prayer and he accepted Jesus Christ as his personal savior and Lord. In conclusion of praying the Salvation prayer I glazed upon his face and his countenance looked very joyful. This is the best, he turns to me and said, "would you like to pray for his two friends as well to accept Jesus Christ as their personal savior and Lord. I was so overwhelmed with joy with this man's level of compassion, in that he received Jesus Christ as his savior, a minute ago and he is willing to share the blessings with his friends to accept the Lord as well. I was sharing the good news with his friends and people who were going into the women restroom, stopped and listen to the gospel of Jesus Christ. I was so excited to know that there is a place all over this world where the good news can be preached, we must get serious about this work. Later, in this book, I will list some places I have led people to Jesus Christ as their personal savior and Lord. God is no respecter of person and I am no respecter of person. I am just doing what God has anointed me to do and to do it with the best of the ability that he has bestowed upon me. I am committed to fulfilling the call of God upon my life.

I know Christ was preach that day, and people heard the good news that very day. Some people literally stop to hear the gospel and it was as if we were having church.

This reminded me of the Bible teachings,

"My command is this: Love each other as I have loved."

John 15:12

"Carry each other's burdens, and in this way, you will fulfill the law of Christ."

Galatians 6:2

"Each of you should look not only to your own interests, but also to the interest of others."

Philippians 2:4

This man just gave his life to Jesus Christ as his savior and he was looking out for the interest of his other friends. This man displayed the look of God and I have decided to place this scenario in this life changing and inspirational book for every reader to placed emphasis on looking people the way God showed his love towards us.

We need to stop playing church and doing church which is loving people and demonstrating the love of God. Too often, church people talk love and do not show it. This man just got saved and showed love in the greatest dimension possible. Freely he received, freely and gave to his friends. God had a divine purpose and time for me being there at the location so that they can be saved and know the true and living God. Thank you, Jesus, for using me in a dynamic way in bringing these three people to you.

May they in turn do the same for as many people as possible that come to use the restrooms and the rest stop. They have a ready ministry ministering to all the people that come their way. May God give them a supernatural anointing to share the good news of Jesus Christ with wisdom, knowledge and power. Look at My God, reader of the awesome work God has given me to do on the earth.

Chapter 11

Outreach 2

Chapter 11
Outreach 2

We are heading closer to our destination, home and we stopped off again to relaxed for a few minutes when suddenly I looked upon a young lady who was not looking like she was doing well. I approached her and asked her, "are you doing good?" She replied by saying, "who wants to know." I replied by saying, my name is Pastor Paul and she looked at me with a wide eye and full of anticipation in her eyes.

I knew that mentioning my name brought some form of solace to her, I am thinking she felt that I will be moved with some form of compassion in either giving her a physical help in the form of money, food or some form of spiritual help.   I did not have any cash to give her. However, I knew she believed that help was coming to her this very moment because the way she looked at me. Therefore, I proceeded to ask her some question, but she was a bit reluctant to answer my questions. We were both trying to break the ice, "so to speak" with our level of conversation.

I shared with her, that Jesus loves you dearly and she smiled and on seeing her smiled I know I was getting through to her. However, she was a bit strong willed and I understood living a life on the street prepared her to be strong and powerful when dealing with people. We engaged in conversation for a few more minutes and she shared with me some things about her life. I knew she was not giving me the whole picture of her being at the gas station peddling money, but I believed she was on either drugs or prostituting herself. I told her, that God loves her and whatever she is doing God is not pleased with it, I did not judge her, but I judged her act, which got her thinking. My reader, you are probably thinking why I am making these statements about this young woman.

The reason for making these statements is due to the fact, I operate in the gifts of the spirit of God. My giftings are in the area of word of knowledge, word of wisdom and discerning of spirit. I have been operating in these gifts for over twenty-six years and most importantly, I operate under the obedience wisdom, guidance of the Holy Spirit.

She did not give her life to Jesus Christ; however, I know the word of God went forth and I pray one day I see her again. I am praying for that woman that God will send someone to minister to her or I will see her again. I know God can help her, if she is willing to get the necessary that will bring into a walk of victory. We just must be willing to do our part to help set the captives free. Remember, God desires that all be saved, and all come into the knowledge of the truth, which is, you must be born-again in order to enter the kingdom of heaven.

Chapter 12

Outreach 3

Chapter 12
Outreach 3

Well, we arrived at home parked the rental car in the garage about 6:45pm and my wife and I, we were tired and hungry. We dropped off our things at home and proceeded to go to a restaurant to get something to satisfy our hunger needs. My wife was feeling for a hamburger and I wanted some fish tacos. We went at one of our favorite burger joint to eat. We ordered our food and waited for the server to serve our food.

While waiting on our food I noticed a young lady I knew as the server. We chatted for a few minutes and I shared the love of Jesus Christ with her. She mentioned to me that, "she is working, and she will pick me up on the offer to accept Jesus Christ the next time we met?" I said, yes and I will hold you to your promise.

My wife looked at me and said, "you do not waste time at all with sharing the gospel." I replied by saying, I may never see some people again, so I take every opportunity to share the gospel with people. She smiled and we were waiting for our meal, while recapping the weekend conference and journey to Santa Cruz.

When suddenly a family came in to order their food, they looked very combative and I said to my wife they look like trouble. They complained about the meal and one of the young men started to get on in an unruly manner. I was praying that God tempered the situation and he kept looking at me and did not pay him any attention. After the older gentleman ate the meal he went to the cashier and complained that the food was terrible, and he wanted his money back. The cashier made a call to the manager and she gave them a back their money after eating most of the meal and they left.

After they left the young lady whom I minister the gospel too, said she will definitely accept Jesus Christ the next time we met, and we ate our meal and said to her and her fellow co-workers take care and be blessed in Jesus name. To my surprised I saw the young lady a couple of weeks later walking down the road on her way to work. I mentioned to her the promise she made with me and she said "yes."

I said to her, would like to accept Jesus Christ as your personal savior and Lord today. She said "yes." I prayed the salvation prayer with her, and she accepted Jesus as her personal savior and Lord.

The Bible teaches,

"And everyone who calls on the name of the Lord will be saved."

Acts 2:21

I see this young lady occasionally and she is doing well, and I get to know her mother as well and they are doing good. I encourage her and her mother to attend a spirit filled Bible believing church. The mother said, "they go to different churches and they are happy knowing the Lord."

Everyone I have led to the Lord Jesus I am praying for them that they walk in God's commands and stature and they live a life that is obedient to God. This book culminates my scenarios of leading people to Jesus Christ on my Santa Cruz journey from Friday 29th December through Sunday 31st 2018.

During that year 2018 the Lord Jesus Christ use me to lead 398 souls all to the glory of God.

I want to encourage all those who desire to be more effective in leading people to Jesus Christ, depend on God's Holy Spirit to empower you and give you the boldness the share the gospel of Jesus Christ.

Remember, God desire

"All people to be saved and to come into the knowledge of the truth."

1 Timothy 2:4

"Jesus replied, "Verily I tell you; no one can see the kingdom of God unless they are born again."

John 3:3

Therefore, if Jesus desire all people to be saved. I will like to see everyone saved as well. Be encourage you can win the lost for Christ too, do not be afraid God will help you accomplish this work. Stay committed to the call of God upon your life. I communicate with a few of the people I led to the Lord in this book via text messages to encourage them to read their Bible regularly and pray every day for strength.

I will like to encourage my reader, take time to know God in an intimate way. Ask the Holy Spirit to give you understanding as you read your Bible. God is calling you into an intimate relationship with Him. May God reveal himself to you in a greater and dynamic dimension and at the end of it all you can say LOOK AT MY GOOD.

Listed below are some of the areas I led people to Jesus Christ as their personal savior and Lord.

- At the Shopping Malls
- Restaurants
- Swimming pools
- Spas
- At the airports
- On airplanes
- At the gyms
- At conferences
- At Supermarket stores
- At the retail stores
- Financial Institutions
- Car dealerships
- Beaches

- At car rentals
- At hotels
- Groceries/Farmers markets
- Fast Food Outlets
- Schools
- Laundry Mart
- Hospitals
- Dry cleaners
- Insurance Offices
- Roadside services
- Motor Vehicles Offices
- Gas Stations
- Dental Offices
- Visionary Offices
- Vet Offices
- Business Meetings

The list my reader can go on and on. There are no limits to where I have led people into a relationship with Jesus Christ. My reader, if it is done by me and it can also be done by you as well. What is require is a committed and dedicated heart to do the work of the Lord and complete it to the end. Remember, God is no respecter of person.

Conclusion

I want to encourage my reader, to take time and seek the Lord for wisdom, knowledge and understanding in winning the lost for Jesus Christ. God has invested a lot for us to be mediocre Christians. We must be on our father's business and go after winning people to Jesus Christ. It's not difficult, however, you must be willing to discipline and focus to the work God has called you to do. People are dying and if they do not know Jesus Christ as their personal savior and Lord, they are eternally separated from their maker.

Let us get serious about ministering to our friends and family members in these last and closing days. If you are willing God will give you the desires of your heart to win the lost, that was my prayer in 1993 and to date God have never disappointed me. I have been winning the lost for the past twenty-six years and it has been a great journey in the Lord. Stay blessed my reader, and you will find tremendous joy doing the work of the Lord.

Qualifications to be Born-Again

Ephesians 2:8-9

For by grace you have saved through faith, and not through anything that you have done. It is a gift from God, and did not come about through working for it, in case anyone wants to boast.

1. Admit you are a sinner, having broken and transgressed against God's laws, and need a savior. Romans 6:23

2. Believe in Jesus Christ as the son of God, who died to pay for our sins. John 3:3 and John 3:16

3. Repent for your sins. Romans 10:9 and 1 John 1:9

4. Accept Jesus Christ as your personal savior and Lord. John 3:3

5. Please direct your attention to the next section and pray the Salvation prayer. The Lord is waiting for you my reader, to come to Him because of His awesome love for you. His arms are wide open to accept you into the body of Christ. He paid the ultimate price for your sins.

He is waiting for your response to Hi, so you may have life more abundantly. Life is too precious to waste, and He will give you a life to your fullest potential in Him. He loves you dearly and is waiting to show you His awesome power in your life and allow you to live in victory because He is the king or Kings and the Lord of Lords.

To the unbeliever and the person who wants to give, or-rededicate their life to Christ, please pray the Salvation prayer on the following page.

If you made a commitment to live for Jesus Christ for the rest of your life, please Email me and let me know of your new birth experience. See my contacts page for more information.

The Salvation Prayer

Dear Jesus Christ,

I come to you just as I am, a sinner and confess all my past and present sins before you. Help me to live a truly Christian life in accordance with your word. From now on, dear God. I will live only for you, by your grace and mercy. Thank you for saving me, in Jesus' name.

If you have prayed this prayer and believe in Christ in your heart. The Bible states that you are now Born- Again.

"I tell you the truth: no one can see the kingdom of God unless he is born-again."

John 3:3

Celebrate your new birth by finding a home church where the undefiled and pure word of God is taught. The Lord will equip, strengthen and encourage you to live a life that is above reproach.

I would like to know that you are being taught well, advancing in the things of God, making valuable contributions to the kingdom, and most importantly, that you are putting to flight demons who are oppressing people.

The Lord will work through you, if you allow Him to do so in the process, therefore don't hesitate to send me an Email and let me know how you are doing. See my contacts page.

We hope that you enjoyed this valuable time of teaching with Pastor Caprietta.

If you would like to contact Pastor Caprietta for additional copies of this book or his other books, schedule a speaking engagement or check his events, please contact:

Pastors Paul and Gail Caprietta

Co-laborers in Christ

<u>www.divineministriesinc,org</u>

Office: 562-806-0969

Email: **Pastorcaprietta@hotmail.com**

Please visit Amazon.com by searching Paul Caprietta and refer friends and family members to these life-changing and inspirational books.

I would like to encourage my reader, to get the followings books by the same author, so that, your knowledge and understanding of winning the lost for Jesus Christ with be strengthen. Please take time to look at some of my books on the following pages. You will find these books to be very helpful and life changing. Your life will never be the same after you read these awesome books.

Take this opportunity to check out these life changing, awesome and inspirational books on the next few pages for your reading pleasure. May God inspire you as you read these books. Thanking you in advance for your support as you advance the work of the Lord.

LOOK AT
MY GOD
Pastor Paul
Caprietta

Look at My God! 2
Victories in Evangelism
Pastor Paul Caprietta

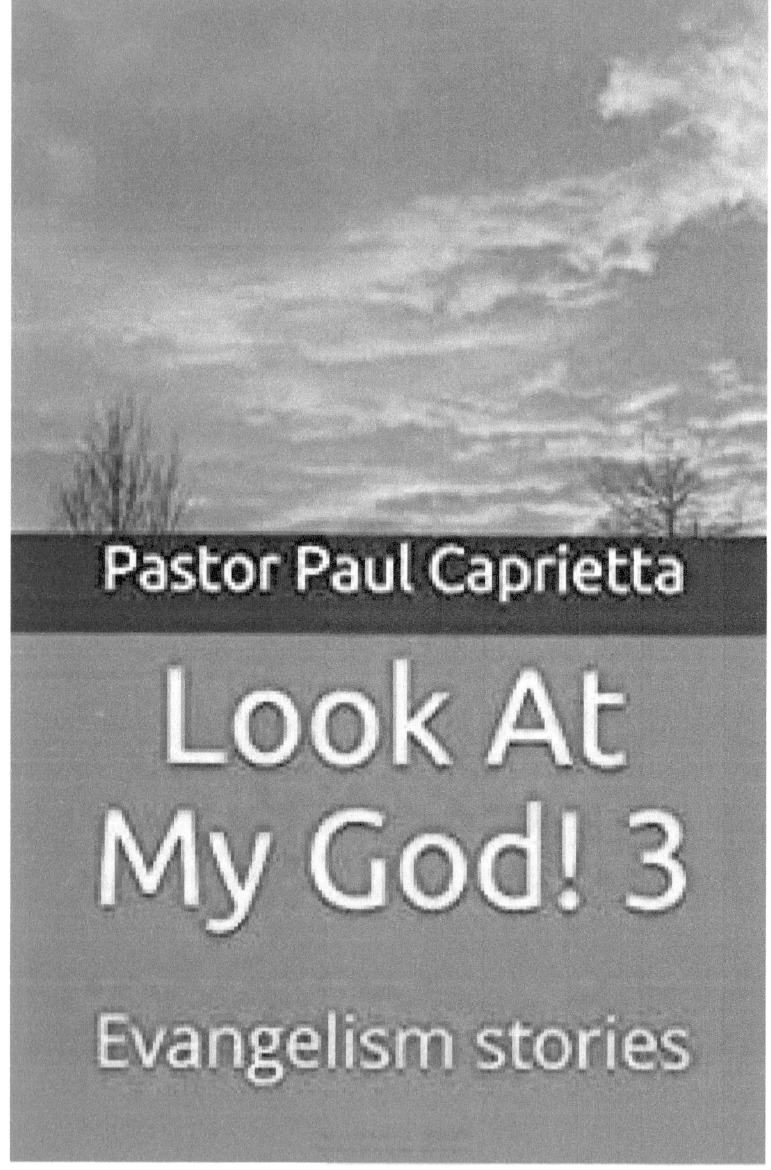
Pastor Paul Caprietta
Look At
My God! 3
Evangelism stories

WE
Serve
An awesome
God
Who loves you?
dearly

WE
Can Do
All Things
Through
Christ
That gives us
Strength

Learn to Put God First in your life

Note Taking

Note Taking

Note Taking